UNSTUCK

A GUIDE TO UNKNOTTING THE TWINES TO SUCCESS

DAVE ALESE

ISBN: 979-8-3303-0511-7

UNSTUCK!

Unless otherwise indicated, all Scripture quotations are taken from the New Living Translation (NLT) of the Bible.

Published by Geans Edge Production

To contact the Author
Email: contact@davealese.com
Website: www.davealese.com

CONTENTS

ACKNOWLEDGEMENTS

This work would not have been a reality without the impact of many great leaders that have poured into me.

To my Pastor of many years, Rev. Victor Adeyemi, thank you for being a spiritual covering for us these many years. Indeed you sowed the seeds of destiny in our hearts as teenagers. Your teachings continue to resonate with me, serving as a constant reminder to serve others and lead with purpose and passion.

To the late Dr. Myles Munroe, though you may not be physically present, your legacy lives on in the hearts of countless individuals, including mine. Your journey has been a beacon of inspiration, showcasing what true leadership and purpose–driven living entail. Thank you for being a remarkable role model and for leaving behind a legacy that continues to impact lives around the globe.

My dearest Adenike and our kids, you all are the pillars of my strength, and the stars that light up my sky. Nike, you're not just the best I could ever ask for, but my partner in every adventure, in every struggle, and my inspiration in every moment. Your consistent support and countless sacrifices have fueled the fire within me to keep chasing this dream of becoming an author.

And to all those who have supported me, whether you've been my cheerleader or giving yourself to be mentored by me, your presence has been invaluable on this journey. This book wouldn't have been possible without each and every one of you.

INTRODUCTION

All over the world, people desire better. Everyone wants continuous progress. Regardless of your current level, there is always a bigger level. It's what we call the next **level.**

God promises us ever continuing increase. The Biblical Book of Proverbs 4 verse 18 in the Message Translation unveils God's plan for our lives as this–

"The longer we live, the brighter we shine"

Ideally, our lives should be on a path of nonstop growth and increase. Whoever saw you yesterday should see obvious improvements today. That is the perfect will of God.

However, a lot of people are stuck. Even though they are well aware that a next level awaits them, they do not know how to make the desired progress and it seems like they are on the same spot perpetually. Like a car stuck in 2nd gear, they simply find it hard to transit and move on. Life just seems like a rough, tough, noisy struggle.

Romans 12 verse 2 says, "And be not conformed to this world: but be ye *transformed* by the renewing of your mind, that ye may prove what is that good, and acceptable, and perfect, will of God." This scripture confirms that though transformation is our best option as a people, this transformation must be ignited from within, taking place first and foremostly in our hearts. The mind must be renewed by taking away the old way of thinking and exchanging it with a new way.

As simple as that sounds, it is hard work. Truthfully, there must be both Deliberate and Consistent efforts in order to achieve that, not a once–and–for–all kind of effort.

In paying close attention to that scripture in Romans, you'll discover that the common word to both 'TRANSFORM' and 'CONFORM' is 'FORM'. In other words, the pattern of our lives is a product of the formation of our minds. That is why Proverbs 4 verse 20–22 says:

> **20** ***My son, pay attention to what I say; turn your ear to my words.***
> **21** ***Do not let them out of your sight, keep them within your heart;***
> **22** ***for they are life to those who find them and health to one's whole body.***

The 24th verse says that "out of the heart are the issues of life".

Indeed, the state of the heart determines how the whole life turns out to be.

As a man thinks in his heart so is he! It all begins with the heart.

In Joshua 1 verse 8, God made it clear to Joshua, that his success was solely dependent on him (Joshua). God's word to Joshua paraphrased, implied that if he needed to change his life, he needed to change his heart. You see, a lot of people want God to change everything for them. They want a transformed life at the wave of a magic wand. They want a Chef to make the food and to also feed them. They fail to realize that even feeding anyone requires some effort from the one being fed except in a totally dependent case of tube–feeding. Even at that, digestion is dependent on the body of the one being fed and not the feeder. Either way, there's a role for everyone to play.

That is why this book is important. It wields powerful principles and revelations on our roles to play that are sure to change anyone's heart and life.

Allow me to announce to you and to every devil that your tomorrow is greater than your today. Far greater! Don't let anyone judge you by your current status; you are still on your way!

2 Corinthians 4 verse 18 in the Message Translation says, "So we don't look at the troubles we can see now; rather, we fix our gaze on things that cannot be seen. For the things we

see now will soon be gone, but the things we cannot see will last forever."

Don't let anyone label you too soon. You may not have it all together now, but you are coming through. You're coming through sooner than you think. Your friends and mates may have gone ahead, but there is room for catching up and even overtaking, as you will quickly discover when you begin to live out the principles of this book.

If you had met Joseph (of the book of Genesis) in Potiphar's house, you would have related to him as a slave. If you had met him in prison after then, you would have called him a prisoner but these transient facts didn't change the truth about his glorious future. That slave/prisoner was a Prime minister in the making, and it didn't matter that all of Egypt wasn't yet aware of it. By the time his time had come to rule in the palace, Egypt and her people succumbed to his leadership regardless of his background as a slave/prisoner. If you had gone back to the same address of his prison cell or his slave quarters a few years after he had left there, you would not have met him there because he would have relocated to his rightful address in the palace.

Do not be apologetic about your circumstances because you are a work–in–progress. Stop looking at anyone else's lane. Focus on your own life's lane and keep on working. Your address will soon change!

Do not let anyone label you by your current job or current car or based on your current bank statement or current house, none of these are a reflection of the future God has designed for you.

If you have ever been to a construction site, you would only see a mess. It usually doesn't look comely or all put together. But I tell you this–if only you visit it again after a while, after a little more work, after a little more effort, after a little more commitment to betterment, when all the debris has been cleared away and the house stands painted in all its glory and the lawn is all made up and the flowers are in full bloom, everyone would want to live there. The project of your life might currently be under construction and while you're laying the bricks, hitting the nails, scraping the floor, and dredging the sewage, it may not be a pretty sight. Don't be discouraged or overwhelmed. You're coming out dazzling! You're on your way to becoming the you that you would always be proud of. Even a 100-storey building was built one floor after the other, one day at a time. All you need to do is to keep at it. The best part is–God's got your back! Don't ever give up and you are guaranteed to finish on top.

I encourage you to read this book with an open heart and to get the most out of it. Be willing to put the principles into practice. Keep it in your library for reference and you may also give out copies to friends, proteges, colleagues, loved ones, and all those who may need it.

I cannot wait to hear your success story!

Welcome to Unstuck!

CHAPTER 1

Success Is A Choice!

> ***"Study this Book of Instruction continually. Meditate on it day and night so you will be sure to obey everything written in it. Only then will you prosper and succeed in all you do."***
>
> Joshua 1:8 (NLT)

Choice is such a powerful word/element

In the scripture above, the power of *personal* choice is clearly magnified as you will notice that your success is more dependent on *you* than it is on God. The passage states that "**You** shall make **thy** way prosperous.... and **you** shall have good success".

God NEVER forces anyone to be or do anything, including being successful. The greatest power God gave man is simply the ability to choose. This gift is so powerful and significant that man has the autonomy to use this power for or against himself and in some cases, even against God Himself who gave this power of choice in the first place. Man can even choose not to have a relationship with God even though God makes this choice available to everyone.

In the Biblical book of Deuteronomy 30:19, these are the words of the covenant which the Lord commanded Moses to make with the children of Israel, presenting choices to the children of Israel and by extension to everyone:

> ***"I call heaven and earth as witnesses today against you, that I have set before you life and death, blessing and cursing; therefore, choose life, that both you and your descendants may live"***

Even though God certainly and relentlessly encourages us to choose life, ultimately, the decision is ours to make. Ours and ours alone. Whoever is interested in making a choice benefits from choosing and choosing right.

If God was to make every single decision for man, he would not be a free agent. God is a gentleman. He won't defile man by denying him the power of choice or by forcing him to do anything. By this, God teaches mankind to be intentional and deliberate about his every action because God Himself is a deliberate and intentional God.

Success defined

What is Success? Is success having a new car? Is it buying a new mansion? Well, success is **none of** those things. Those are simply the benefits or fruits of success and not the 'tree' of success itself.

Success is primarily finding your purpose and fulfilling it. You can say you are succeeding in life when you keep maximizing your potential.

The Reward of Success

Finding that one thing that even if you wouldn't be paid for it, you would still do it gladly–this is the reward for success. This is the reason why work is fun for truly successful people.

Successful people work harder than anyone else because it foremostly brings them fulfillment. It's such a joy to them. Not having to do it makes them uneasy. At this point in the journey of purpose, **Success is its own reward.** When success becomes its own reward, chasing your purpose and giving yourself to it completely will be relatively easy.

That said, no one stumbles on success. Being successful means being extra intentional and extra deliberate. Every successful person that I have met or read about chose to be successful and stayed committed, intentional and deliberate about paying the price for success. This tells us that the pathway to success is pretty predictable and this is largely courtesy of certain landmarks along that pathway called 'Principles' or 'Laws'. Life itself is guided by Principles.

A key would open a door to whoever uses it, even if it's not the house owner. Even if the person is a child, as long as the correct keys are in use, the key delivers without prejudice. The door has no choice but to become unlocked. The right key gives you command over any given situation.

> ***"And I will give you the*** *keys* ***of the Kingdom of Heaven. Whatever you forbid on earth will be forbidden in heaven, and whatever you permit on earth will be permitted in heaven."***
>
> Matthew 16:19 (NLT)

Knowledge is a key–

> ***"What sorrow awaits you experts in religious law! For you remove the*** *key* ***to knowledge from the people. You don't enter the Kingdom yourselves, and you prevent others from entering."***
>
> Luke 11:52 (NLT)

Principles are Keys. Laws are Keys.

God sets principles in motion so that everyone can leverage them equally at any age and from anywhere around the world. This is why, till eternity, principles are no respecter of persons or locations. They deliver excellently regardless of by whom or where it is engaged. Principles and Laws are so critical that they can either make or mar one's life. If, for example, a little child mistakenly plunges into a pool without knowing how to swim, the law of flotation would be flouted, and this could kill the child. Meanwhile, the same law, when properly applied, aids the smooth sailing of great ships on the sea.

Seeing that success is guided by principles, this means that life itself is pretty predictable. Once the principles or laws are obeyed, eventual success is guaranteed.

Bear in mind that throughout this book, the terms 'laws' and 'principles' will be used interchangeably to refer to the same thing.

Be open to carefully following the laws of success to come and you're on your way to becoming a success yourself!

LET'S SAY THIS TOGETHER:

"I choose to be a Success! Success is God's intent and purpose for my life!"

CHAPTER 2

THE LAW OF PURPOSE

"I knew you before I formed you in your mother's womb. Before you were born, I set you apart and appointed you as my prophet to the nations".

Jeremiah 1:5 (NLT)

God never starts anything until He has finished it first.

I'll say that again.

God never starts anything until He has finished it first.

The fact of your existence is solid proof that God has a complete plan for your life. The fact that you showed up on the scene shows that He has already finished writing your script.

God is making something beautiful with our lives.

Joseph the 'Dreamer' may have been *sold* into slavery but the truth according to God's completed plan for his life was that he was *sent* to Egypt to preserve lives, even the lives of those who sold him into slavery.

Going forward, please believe that there's something great about your life no matter what.

Please believe from today that your life is greatness steadily unfolding. Why?

If you had met Moses when he ran away from Egypt, you would have called him a murderer and a fugitive but this didn't change the fact that he was created to be the leader of the greatest nation. Regardless of all that happened in his youth, he was made to be the commander in chief of Israel under God their King.

This is why no matter how hard the devil tries and no matter the situation you're faced with, once you wake up each morning, you should boldly tell him to his face, "you won't keep me here", "you cannot keep me here because God has a bigger picture and a better plan for me and I'm definitely going with that!".

Hit the ground running. Hit the ground praying and declaring God's word to you. Hit the ground working!

The New Testament of the Holy Scriptures shares a couple of testimonies in this regard.

The devil kept Lazarus in the cold arms of death for a few days, but when Jesus showed up, Lazarus became under new management–The Resurrection and the Life! The devil and death had no choice but to let him go!

The impotent man by the pool of Siloam had been there for 38 years until Jesus showed up.

The blind man by the Beautiful Gate had been there for a mighty long time until Peter showed up in the power of God and the rest, they say, is history.

Tell the devil again, "Satan, guess what? Jesus showed up!!"

Jesus is showing up for you!

Hallelujah!

Living on Purpose

We all are blessed by God to succeed in life because we are all gifts from Him to our world. Every single one of us. None of us was created to fail or created to be an empty wanderer.

This is why you must never think of yourself as someone who has nothing. Jesus told the parable of the rich man who gave gifts to his servants. Though the gifts were in different measures, everyone had *something*. You too have something!

While believing that we are all blessed with something precious is a matter of perspective and insight, knowing what to do with what we have all kicks off from the heart. This is what purpose is about–discovering what your life is meant for right from your heart where God dwells.

Genesis 1:26–28 (NLT) made it clear that God had a purpose in mind when He made man–

> ***"Then God said, "Let us make human beings in our image, to be like us. They will reign over the fish in the sea, the birds in the sky, the livestock, all the wild animals on the earth,and the small animals that scurry along the ground." So God created human beings in his own image. In the image of God he created them; male and female he created them. Then God blessed them and said, "Be fruitful and multiply. Fill the earth and govern it. Reign over the fish in the sea, the birds in the sky, and all the animals that scurry along the ground."***

Of a truth, whenever Purpose is not known, abnormal–use or abuse is inevitable. In fact, abuse is mandatory.

A life without purpose can never amount to anything because it's going nowhere.

Everyone features in the grand plan of God. We are all actors in the movie written by God.

Until your role is played, you can't die or leave the scene. When your Purpose is revealed to you, it will set a vision in your heart for you to live for.

The Bible says in Proverbs 29:18 (NLT):

> ***"When people do not accept divine guidance, they run wild. But whoever obeys the law is joyful."***

This means that without vision, people don't know what to say 'yes' to and what to say 'no' to because everything seems right and everywhere looks like the final destination.

There may be several exits on the highway but vision and purpose work hand–in–hand to determine which one you take. They pair up to keep you in check and discipline you along the way.

Paul the Apostle said in the book of 1 Corinthians 10:23 (NLT), "You say, "I am allowed to do anything"–but not everything is good for you. You say, "I am allowed to do anything"–but not everything is beneficial."

This means some things may be legal to do but not all those

things are beneficial. Living according to vision and living according to purpose will prune our lives of unnecessary distractions and excesses.

How do I find Purpose?

Find God: He had something in mind while He was forming you. He alone holds the purpose for your creation and further existence because He made/manufactured you.

Through your design: This also offers hints of your purpose. What do you find so easy to do? Speaking? Creating things? Designing? Planning? What are you gifted at? What is that thing that when you do it, you get the most sense of joy and fulfillment as well as the most praise from people? Your personality traits, your physical makeup, and your character uniqueness were all wired in by God as pointers to your purpose/function. It's all a part of His plan.

As long as you're in your own lane and in your own race, keep putting in the work and you are bound to succeed. Never try to win in a race you are not called to run in because progress is not in the speed but the *direction*.

LET'S SAY THIS TOGETHER:

"Going forward, I walk in purpose and function according to God's blueprint, God's design and God's vision for me"

CHAPTER 3

THE LAW OF VISION

"It was by faith that Moses left the land of Egypt, not fearing the king's anger. He kept right on going because he kept his eyes on the one who is invisible."

Hebrews 11:27 (NLT)

Vision is seeing what could be.

Vision is seeing what is not as though it were.

Vision is seeing potential in the future even in the midst of contradictory circumstances.

Vision is literally seeing the invisible.

Vision is that which though others do not see it yet, it is very, very real in your heart. It has become so tangible and has taken form within you.

You cannot go further than where you are until you can see further than where you are.

Moses was described in the verse above as *keeping his eyes on the invisible.* Little wonder he was able to do the impossible. It takes seeing the invisible to do the impossible.

I believe that for every miracle and strange act of God that Moses did, he had seen the pictures in his heart. It had already come to pass in his heart and he was, as it were, walking into his vision. He walked into the picture on his inside and grew his person on the outside into that person on the inside who perfectly fits into that vision.

God cannot do much with us if we are not willing to catch a vision, first of all, in our hearts.

This is one of the most powerful forces in all the efforts to jolt us out of being UNSTUCK and launch us forward as we journey through life.

Life is bigger than buying a good car or living in a good

house. It's way bigger. How about owning several hundreds or thousands of houses for thousands of families to live in? Now that's a vision to catch!

There's a key to activating and enjoying that kind of unlimited resource from God. The Key is the Law of Vision. Our vision must grow and by growing, I mean it must grow and match up with God's big picture. Our focus must change. We earnestly need to shift our focus from just thinking of the little things we want to eat and drink and wear and drive. We must start thinking of how to own manufacturing plants and industries that will provide jobs for tens or hundreds of thousands of people in order to get them on their own journeys towards significance. When you arrive at this new focus and your vision is all grown up, even your prayer points would change. At this point, God says to your prayers, 'Now, you're talking!'. I imagine He even points you out to His angels and says, 'That is my child praying, my son in whom I am well pleased! He talks big and global just like Me'.

God gave Jesus so He could gain the whole world back to Himself. God always thinks BIG. He always has a big picture in mind. Be like **God.** Think Big. Think Big for the sake of millions around the world!

It's interesting to note that most of the time, where we are may not look anything like our vision.

In Gen. 1:1–3 (KJV), all God saw was darkness and emptiness. There is an adjective in the scripture that describes the darkness as *gross* darkness meaning there was no ray of light whatsoever. It was all Pitch Black. The Bible says the earth was "void" which means it was totally empty. Yet, in the midst of darkness and nothingness, God saw the possibility of a substance called 'light' and He called it forth. He ignored the darkness and focused on the picture of the earth He saw on the inside and declared what He wanted to see.

There is such a principle called the **Principle of Double Creation**. It says that 'everything in life is created twice; first in the invisible or spiritual world and then it was created in the physical'. Think about it–every invention you see today, including cars, airplanes, telephones, computers and the like, all first started as thoughts in the minds of the inventors.

Once upon a time, they never existed in the physical. They were first available in the thought realm.

They were first **Ideas.**

They were first **Pictures.**

They were first **Visions.**

Today, they are everywhere and can be handled physically. With this, you can understand that the invisible world is not just as real as the visible world, it, in fact, controls it.

Ephesians 3:20 tells us that God is well able to bring to pass not only all that we ask for but also all that we think/imagine/

dream.

It is important to have a dream. It is, however, more important to have a good, big dream because dreams are empty cheques and you can and should fill in as much as you can because they will be brought to pass.

God employs the power of Vision in His dealings with man. In Genesis 15:5, God took Abraham outside to see the stars of the sky in order to assure him that he would have an uncountable number of descendants even though he and his wife had been childless all their married lives and were both way past childbearing age. God knew Abraham needed to conceive this possibility in his mind before it can become his reality in such a unique circumstance as theirs. In order for this to happen, God shared the vision He had predestined for Abraham using things he could relate with such as countless stars of the sky. God showed him the vision again in Genesis 22:17 saying, "In blessing I will bless you, and multiplying I will multiply your descendants as the stars of heaven and as the sand which is on the seashore; and your descendants shall possess the gate of their enemies". God gave him the vision again using the sand on the seashore until he caught the vision.

Filmmakers and TV producers understand how vision casting impacts the human mind which is why a lot of futuristic ideas and ideals are first introduced in big–budget films and TV series long before they are implemented for real. These professionals realize that the more we conceptualize ideas in visual form, the more we inadvertently acclimatize with them and the easier it is to accept those ideas or ideals as a societal norm. Think tele–'vision'.

The story behind the creation of Disney World is a classic tale of vision that I just must add here, howbeit summarily:

While Disney World is one happy and magical place nearly everyone hopes to visit at least once in their lifetime, this dreamland was all the dream of a man named Walt.

Walt Disney's childhood was unique. He was said to fantasize a lot about art during classes, drawing up sketches throughout most lessons and not completing school with the greatest of grades. He continued to improve on his talent in art creation though, taking correspondence courses and night classes because he hoped to own a storytelling empire. Having his fair share of the ups and downs faced by business startups through the 1930s and 1940s, Walt Disney quickly became an animation favorite, winning several awards for his stellar stories about Mickey Mouse as well as Snow White and the Seven Dwarfs. Walt suffered a nervous breakdown in the same period due to overwork and contract losses. By the 1940s, he was neck–deep in debt and unable to fully fund staff salaries due to the Second World War. Still, Walt continued to seek ways to expand the Disney business. At the time, he was getting letters from happy kids all over the world asking to visit Walt Disney Studios. Then he thought–what if he created a theme park that could keep kids and adults happy?

He traveled the world, visiting theme park after theme park, doing research. Walt then opened the 160–acre Disneyland theme park for business in 1955 at Orange County, California. It became a massive hit and in four years, he seeks to expand again. He heads east and starts buying up land in Orlando, Florida. Walt planned to use it to build a bigger and better version of Disneyland. In 1965, Walt announced his plans for his big dream called Walt Disney World which he visualized as a destination with golf courses, hotels, and shopping experiences. In all, he envisioned a perfect, happy place in Florida.

Sadly, Walt died in 1966. His brother Roy stepped up to fill his shoes and completed his dream calling it Walt Disney World. Walt Disney World's Magic Kingdom opened in 1971 and the park at the fun universe could fit the Disneyland theme park in just its parking lot with extra room to spare.

Disney World is the success Walt dreamed it would be and perhaps even more. Even though he wasn't alive to see it become a must–see dreamland for families all over the world, he visualized this wonderland so much that it felt so real to him. He 'lived' in the vision even though he didn't see it. His vision was so clearly spelt out that it could easily be carried out by his brother after his death. That is the power of Vision!

The Audacity of Vision

There's an extraordinary kind of audacity you carry as a result of having a vision. As an aftermath of catching the vision, Abraham and Sarah agreed with God and changed the names they've always been known as for almost 100 years to the names that suit the vision. You can imagine how people must have been making fun of them whenever they called themselves by their new names. Abraham–the father of multitudes. Sarah–the mother of nations. What a contradiction to their physical status of barrenness at the ages of 90 & 70! Eventually, their vision became their reality.

In the book of Genesis, Joseph had a vision of leadership even though his circumstances appeared to be otherwise. He was the bullied and ignored sibling, he was the slave and later in life, he was the prisoner. Though along his journey, several people mocked him his brothers stole his special coat of many colors, threw him into a pit, sold him off into slavery, lied that he was dead, accused him of molestation then eventually sent him to jail, **they could not take away his dreams**. He protected the vision of his heart and even though he went through hell and high waters, no one could take this vision from him.

When your vision is so great and is a far cry from your present status, certain people are sure to mock you. They will not be able to comprehend how you think your dreams will come true. They may not think you match the picture or fit the bill. They may even call you funny names like 'Joseph the Dreamer' but that's okay. That's who you truly are, the dreamer. Have you caught a vision or a dream from God that has empowered you with the audacity to change your 'name', your way of thinking, and your lifestyle as a whole? Just keep dreaming and working at it, eventually, they will bow to you as they bowed to Joseph when his big dreams came to pass.

1 Samuel's story of David is yet another example of vision at work. Little David was confronted by the huge Goliath, yet David saw the possibility of victory so much that he spoke of victory only.

You need to read the book of 1 Samuel 17:4–5 again in order to fully understand the enormity of the giant before the young Israelite. Goliath was 9 feet tall and his helmet alone weighed 125 pounds (57kg). Nobody wears a cap that is too heavy for one of his arms to remove. It meant that Goliath could easily wear and remove a helmet weighing 125 pounds. Imagine that for a minute! Just picture his massive arms using his helmet as a yardstick. He was a giant, no doubt!

How do you think David would have felt in front of this intimidating creature? Little wonder Saul, the king of Israel, and his entire army were so terrified that no one dared to go head–to–head against this monster for several weeks until David showed up.

Right in the middle of this nerve–wracking national–scaled terrorist attack, David said he would kill Goliath and would also overcome the entire army of the Philistines. What an AUDACITY! What gave him this kind of audacity? Vision. David had received a clear vision and this vision came pouring out of his lips. David must have had such a vivid revelation in his heart of how he was going to overcome this monster with the help of the Lord that he just couldn't shake it off. He had the mental picture. This was why he recalled the picture of how he killed the lion and the bear. He captured the vision of him taking down Goliath so much that it became tangible enough to walk right through. I can imagine that those scenes were playing repeatedly in his mind while he was thinking about Goliath. He was seeing Goliath before his eyes, quite alright, but he already had an inner vision captured with the eyes of his heart about what would become of that enemy. He saw the truth. Vision is the truth!

The Power of Vision

What will having Vision do to and for you?

Vision makes you think about the possibilities that can be: It is a revealer of possibilities.

Vision helps you focus on the benefits and rewards of purposeful actions: It doesn't focus on the presence of problems but on the joy of finding a solution. This is seen here in Verse 25 of 1 Samuel 17 (NLT) as the royal reward of the man who conquers Goliath is described– "Have you seen the giant?" the men asked. "He comes out each day to defy Israel. The king has offered a huge reward to anyone who kills him. He will give that man one of his daughters for a wife, and the man's entire family will be exempted from paying taxes!"

Vision enables you to draw strength from previous similar situations: This was David's courage booster as seen in 1 Samuel 17:34–37 (NLT)–But David persisted. "I have been taking care of my father's sheep and goats," he said. "When a lion or a bear comes to steal a lamb from the flock, I go after it with a club and rescue the lamb from its mouth. If the animal turns on me, I catch it by the jaw and club it to death. I have done this to both lions and bears, and I'll do it to this pagan Philistine, too, for he has defied the armies of the living God! The Lord who rescued me from the claws of the lion and the bear will rescue me from this Philistine!"

Note, though, that Vision may employ the same strategy but a different methodology.

Vision enforces discipline: If you ever see anyone who lives carelessly, it is usually due to the lack of a strong and compelling vision for their lives. People lack restraints or act foolishly when vision is missing.. Proverbs 29:18 (KJV) buttresses this point–"Where there is no revelation, the people cast off restraint". Vision compels you. It forces you to do the needful.

Vision motivates you: It made Joseph become so dedicated to his pursuit of excellence in wisdom that he eventually taught the elders of Egypt (see the proof of this in Psalms 105:22). Because you can see what others cannot, you are therefore willing to do what others aren't willing to do to go the extra mile and get outstanding results.

How do I catch a Vision?

God: Get God. He will open your eyes to what you should be seeing, believing, and becoming. He will give you a vision truly worth chasing with your life. According to the Biblical book of Jeremiah 1:5 (NLT), God told the prophet Jeremiah this: "I knew you before I formed you in your mother's womb. Before you were born, I set you apart and appointed you as my prophet to the nations." God has the same opinion about you. Before you were born, God had an appointment for your whole life.

Reading & Exposure: Refuse to stay small. We are often limited just because you're simply unaware of certain possibilities. However, The inspiration and the power to have new perspectives and catch a vision will come when you see what others have done and when you read stories about how their vision became reality. Remember that there's no vision in darkness. Likewise, there's no vision in ignorance. Illuminate your soul. Get some knowledge and exposure. It floods your being with brightness and ignites the 'Lightbulb moments' needed to drive your vision. Read and meditate on good books starting with the Bible. They say when you rise again after falling or failing, at that point you don't begin from scratch, you begin from experience. How about learning from the failures and successes of great men and women? Begin from their experience. Leverage on their wealth of knowledge. Stand on the shoulders of giants. Read amazing books. Go to amazing places!

Service: The great man David in the Bible gives a sterling example of vision being one of the rewards of service. The lad David was simply serving his father and tending a few sheep faithfully when his opportunity to defeat lions and bears came which became a precursor to the defeat of Goliath. David was only serving his brothers on the battlefield when his opportunity came to be the champion of Israel. This same David was at the backside of the desert and shepherding sheep when his fame and history of service went ahead of him to the palace, creating a space for him to become one of Israel's finest royals. The vision of his life continued to expand and grow clearer as he continued to serve. Serve. Just serve. You expand in capacity as you serve. Also, you just never know who is noticing. Best of all, God is taking note of your faithfulness in serving humanity. Make good use of what you have in serving others. Indeed, it's not what we do not have that limits us but what we have and do not know how to use. Discover how to use what you do have in talents, gifts or products and commit to a life of service and vision will begin to crystalize in your heart.

It is also noteworthy to know that vision usually thrives in your tested and confident environment or your atmosphere of empowerment: That place where you draw strength from. Never allow difficult situations to have you cornered in their atmosphere of fear, doubt and panic rather, always bring your difficult situations into your own environment. It disarms and strips the difficulties of their intimidating power and reduces it in size. Your place of empowerment may be Worship or Prayer. Surround difficult situations with your environment of empowerment and you're sure to make headway.

Never forget that provision only follows vision. This means your supplies are tied to your purpose & vision therefore to live in abundant provision, you have to catch your vision.

Be rest assured that GOD's WILL is always GOD's BILL. He won't make provisions for visions. He did not originate but once you're at work in God's vision for you. His provision will follow you.

LET'S SAY THIS TOGETHER:

"The eyes of my heart receive a God–given vision and I diligently evolve all that I see".

CHAPTER 4

THE LAW OF DILIGENCE

"You are the salt of the earth. But what good is salt if it has lost its flavor? Can you make it salty again? It will be thrown out and trampled underfoot as worthless."

Matthew 5:13 (NLT)

We are the salt of the earth. Jesus called his disciples and by extension, all believers "the salt of the earth".

It is scientifically proven that when iodized salt is exposed to several days of sunlight, impurities, and atmospheric elements, it may still look as shiny as salt but it begins to lose its power and salting strength. Soon enough, it would be simply referred to as a glistening cluster of grainy particles because once it loses its fundamental salty characteristic, it can no longer be referred to as salt, and neither can it be confidently used as salt. When this happens, its saltiness cannot be restored and hence it must and should be thrown out as it can gain high toxic levels, becoming harmful and poisonous if ingested.

Our relevance, fulfillment, and success go hand–in–hand with our willingness to get to work. The moment we begin to derive pleasure from fluttering around doing next to nothing, we begin to lose our essence as the salt of the earth. This is what the scriptures meant when Jesus made an inference to salt losing its flavor. It has thereby lost its main purpose or essence.

You may be called salt but until you jump into that pot of hot sauce and begin your work, you will never fulfill your true purpose as salt. It gets worse when loafing around begins to diminish your inherent saltiness. Find yourself a hot pot of purpose soup and serve your essence to the world, nice and sweet!

No matter what happens, refuse to laze around. Put your strength and time into the right causes. Be thirsty for a life of significance.

Though we were made for relevance and not mere survival, relevance sure does not come automatically. It comes by diligence.

The Bible says:

> ***"The hand of the diligent will rule, But the negligent and lazy will be put to forced labor."***
>
> Proverbs 12:24 (AMP)

The NLT Translation of the same passage says:

> ***"Work hard and become a leader; be lazy and become a slave."***

Scriptures also say in Proverbs 22:29–Seest thou a man who is diligent in his ways, he shall stand before kings, he shall not stand before mean (mere) men.

Diligence is not a gift. Diligence is not a talent. It cannot be wished or fasted for or gotten by prayer. It is achieved by rolling up your sleeves and putting in some good old hard work.

Talent and Gifts will be in vain without diligence. Endowment without diligence comes to nothing.

In 1 Corinthians 15:10 (NLT), Paul said, "But whatever I am now, it is all because God poured out his special favor on me–and not without results. For I have worked harder than any of the other apostles; yet it was not I but God who was working through me by his grace."

Grace, no matter how much, remains in vain in the life of a

lackadaisical man.

What is Diligence?

It is defined by Vocabulary.com. as:

"Doing something thoroughly and well. It's the opposite of doing it lazily or shoddily. If you are tireless and persevering and you **do** things with great care, then you **do** things **diligently**. This is an adverb that goes with hard and careful work."

Diligence is hard work.

In the scriptural verse of John 9:4, even Jesus said He must work –

> ***"I must work the works of Him who sent Me while it is day; the night is coming when no one can work."***

We, therefore, must also work.

Hard work is not a curse. Salvation is not an excuse for living a life devoid of hard work.

You may have great faith but faith cannot replace work. Faith without works is dead.

Faith is in vain without hard work.

Diligence is a requirement for success. This lifelong principle cannot be ignored or wished away.

Why is Diligence so important?

It requires diligence to obey God: Obedience is hard work. In Deuteronomy 28:1, God instructed the people of Israel to hearken *diligently* in order for them to become *above all nations of the earth*. God's instructions in diligence will always cost you, (just ask Abraham who was told to leave everything behind to go to a place God would show him) but the benefits make it worthwhile.

To lead, you must be diligent yourself: Proverbs 12:24 (AMP) says, "The hand of the diligent will rule, But the negligent and lazy will be put to forced labor." Only diligent people can become true leaders. You cannot rule your world if you are not diligent and you certainly cannot effectively influence others without it.

Diligence is required to escape decay: "By much slothfulness the building decayeth; and through idleness of the hands the house droppeth through."–Ecclesiastes 10:18 (KJV) Any house that is thoroughly neglected will eventually decay. Every blessing comes with responsibility. How's that? To get a clear picture, ask a nursing mother or an owner of a car.

No one can escape poverty without diligence: Proverbs 24:30–34 describes the field of a lazy person as 'overgrown with thorns' and unkempt. Thanks to a little sleep and a little slumber, he is thrown into deep poverty and alarming need. Indolence only breeds poverty and nothing more. Prosperity requires diligence. Hard work and labor must become your friend if you want to rule and prosper. The most prosperous men are the most hardworking/smart working.

It takes diligence to achieve excellence and gain mastery: In 1 Corinthians 15:9–10 (NLT), Paul said:

> ***"For I am the least of all the apostles. In fact, I'm not even worthy to be called an apostle after the way I persecuted God's church. But whatever I am now, it is all because God poured out his special favor on me–and not without results. For I have worked harder than any of the other apostles; yet it was not I but God who was working through me by his grace."***

Paul the Apostle said that he labored abundantly than them all (the rest of the apostles) no matter how many they were and how many years they had spent in ministry before he got saved at all. He strived hard to serve the Lord even in difficulty. Paul worked his way from the back and the bottom to become one of the most famed and resultful Apostles of the Lord Jesus to the glory of God. With diligence, the last can become the first. Without diligence, the first can become the last as grace can be on a man in vain. To excel and get ahead, make being diligent a core habit.

Key areas of Diligence

Be diligent about your spiritual advancement

In the word: You must commit yourself to the word and labor in it. Once the word of God dwells in you richly, you won't fall in the day of adversity. The word is your shock absorber and is both your defense and attacking tool against the enemy.

Laboring in prayers: Romans 12:11–12 (NLT)–"Never be lazy, but work hard and serve the Lord enthusiastically.Rejoice in our confident hope. Be patient in trouble, and keep on praying."

Be diligent in stewardship and service

Give everything in serving God. As is said by Jesus in Matthew 22:36–37, surrender your whole being to His service and pleasure. Just as in Psalm 63:8, let your soul follow God closely. Serve God will all that you are and He will uphold you on your path to being successful. He is more interested in making a success out of you than you are about making yourself one. As you may notice, while you serve God, 99 percent of the time, serving humanity plays out alongside.

Be diligent in your assignment/purpose

Even if you haven't found your assignment yet, Ecclesiastes 9:10 declares that whatever your hand finds to do must be done with all your might.

James Garfield, the 20th President of the US entered the University system as a Janitor before he became a Lecturer and then a Professor and then a Dean, and then he worked up to becoming the US president. "If you're too big to do the small things, you're too small to do the big things."

Certain factors are consistently anti–diligence. Let's explore some of them next.

Enemies of diligence

The love of all pleasure and no work: Proverbs 21:17 (NLT) expressly says that "He who loves pleasure shall be poor"

Wrong association: Keeping a close relationship with lazy naysayers will weaken your resolve to be diligent. They will make you look like you're being too hard on yourself when you put in the required work for success. These are mediocre–thinkers. Steer clear from their path for your own good and the good of your purpose.

Hanging on past glory or success: If your best is in your past, then your future is in jeopardy. You must labor consistently and persistently to be a better version of your great self.

Diligence is a choice and not a gift. You must choose to allow Purpose and Vision to keep you diligently on your toes. Those who run from hard work run from greatness.

The best part of diligence is that God is a helper and He is willing to enable us to do what we are *committed* to doing.

LET'S SAY THIS TOGETHER:

"I refuse to be negligent. Rather, I give myself wholly to becoming a diligent person.

CHAPTER 5

THE LAW OF GIVING

"Jesus said, "How can I describe the Kingdom of God? What story should I use to illustrate it?It is like a mustard seed planted in the ground. It is the smallest of all seeds,but it becomes the largest of all garden plants; it grows long branches, and birds can make nests in its shade."

Mark 4:30–32 (NLT)

The principle of giving is equated with the Principle of seed sowing. This is what makes the Principle of Giving one of the most powerful forces on earth. We see it in effect right from the very beginning of life as we know it.

In the prehistoric times of Noah, God said in Genesis 8:22, "For as long as the earth remains, seed time & harvest … shall not cease".

Proverbs 11:25 also says that "A generous man will prosper. He that refreshes others will be refreshed". While we all like to be refreshed, most times, we may find refreshing others as the hardest thing to do even though this is what brings refreshment as the Bible reveals.

Giving to others sets in motion a cycle of sowing and reaping. Any farmer who doesn't sow and yet expects to reap is easily the most foolish farmer in existence.

Giving and being benevolent opens us up to abundance like nothing else.

We see a unique take on the act of giving from the popular biblical story of the Good Samaritan as relayed in Luke 10:30–35 by the Lord Jesus–

> ***"Then Jesus answered and said: "A certain man went down from Jerusalem to Jericho, and fell among thieves, who stripped him of his clothing, wounded him, and departed, leaving him half dead. Now by chance a certain priest came down that road. And when he saw him, he passed by on the other side. Likewise, a Levite, when he***

> ***arrived at the place, came and looked, and passed by on the other side. But a certain Samaritan, as he journeyed, came where he was. And when he saw him, he had*** *compassion*. ***So, he went to him and bandaged his wounds, pouring on oil and wine; and he set him on his own animal, brought him to an inn, and took care of him. On the next day, when he departed, he took out two denarii,*** *gave* ***them to the innkeeper, and said to him, 'Take care of him; and whatever more you spend, when I come again, I will repay you.'"***

From the story above, it is revealed that giving is not a default attribute that results from the fact that you know God, neither is it a fruit of the Spirit. Giving, as a deed, is compelled by personal concern and consideration. Giving is fueled by compassion. The act of giving is driven by the heart of giving. This is what the priest and the Levite were missing; the heart of giving. Compassion. The Samaritans, in scriptural times, were often cast off by the people of Israel as a mixed–race who didn't know the true God but according to this story above, only the Samaritan displayed the character of God.

The Bible says in John 3:16 that, "For God *so loved* the world that He gave His only begotten Son, that whosoever believes in Him should not perish but have everlasting life."

Four distinct mindsets about the act of Giving

In every scene of life, you notice 4 kinds of people with 4

distinct mindsets:

The "Takers": They believe, "what is yours is mine, I will get it". These kinds of people only feel a sensation of care when they receive and this evolves into an entitlement 'Pro Max' mentality. They will get what belongs to others by nook or by crook, by nagging or by crying. Their favorite sentences begin with 'me, myself and I' and they don't have the word 'giving' existent in their life dictionaries. We were all born with this self–centered tendency as an offshoot of the nature of the fallen man and of sin. This tendency is noticeable even in toddlers and they are only taught as they grow that giving is also a sign of love and not just receiving. A lot of us, especially Christians, grow up and change that mentality for the most part while some others remain 'robbers' to varying degrees.

The "Hoarders": They believe, "what is mine is mine, I will keep it". This describes a vast majority of us. There's a story of a father who bought fries for his kid and wanted to take some of the fries later on but the kid didn't want him to. In actuality, the father didn't *need* the fries; he could actually get his own since he not only bought the fries himself but gave them to the kid out of his own will. He simply wanted to share. This mentality sometimes plays out in our relationship with the giver of all, **God**. He willingly gives us life, time, talents, gifts, resources, funds, and sometimes, we unconsciously enter the mentality of being a keeper even toward Him just as in the story cited above. Certainly, at times like those, God would wonder who gave us 'the fries' in the first place?

The Givers: They believe, "what is mine is yours, I will give it". These folks love to share what they believe they own with others. The following are the thought processes behind this mentality:

a. What happens if I don't give it is that my heart becomes seared and it becomes almost impossible for me to ever become a giver.

b. What happens if I give it is that my heart is kept pure and so, it gets easier and easier to give next time.

The Caretakers: They believe, 'what is mine is not really mine, I am only given to manage it." You will be the most willing to give if you are well aware that the resources weren't yours to own in the first place. With this mentality, you understand that it was given to you to keep till the original owner and giver is in need of it. This is the mentality of high–flyers, world shakers, philanthropic moguls and the children of the Most High God. If being 'blessed to be a blessing' were persons on two feet, this was them.

How would you feel if you sent a gift package out for delivery and the courier, instead of taking it to the recipient, decided to take it home for himself? You would be upset because it wasn't meant for him. He was just a courier. Now, imagine how God feels when we don't disburse that which is put in our care to manage for the greater good of many.

The Caretakers see themselves as God's couriers. They know

that everything they have was given to them by God for *His* purpose.

Now, of the 4 kinds of people with 4 distinct mindsets, which of them do you think God would make the most affluent and most successful? The Managers. Absolutely!

The finality of all things is that no one will go to the grave with any possessions. It's best to either distribute all that God has put under your care while you are living to ensure it is well allocated or make plans for future distribution to cater for it when you are gone.

Checks to make when giving…

These are a few thoughts or questions to ask when giving to a cause:

Can I also give more than money? Can I also give my time, efforts and expertise?

What are the motives behind this cause?

Is this organization truly impactful and making a difference?

Does the leadership have the competence and character to maximize my giving?

A heart of giving can be cultivated based on knowledge and understanding. With this, even if it feels like giving takes from you at the moment, you have an understanding that giving actually adds to you and your generations after you because to give is to sow a seed. To sow a seed is to plant a tree. To plant a tree is to reap its fruits and gain more seeds. Giving is a bankable multiplier that puts you years and years ahead. Give today.

LET'S SAY THIS TOGETHER:

"I am a giver to nations and yet I will never lack. From now on, I include giving in my plans and I will reap the fruits of being a giver"

CHAPTER 6

THE LAW OF PLANNING

Life's outcomes must never be left to Chance.

Everything people become **LATER**, they prepared for it **EARLIER**.

The beauty of planning is seen in Proverbs 24:3–4 (NLT):

> ***3 A house is built by wisdom and becomes strong through good sense.***
> ***4 Through knowledge its rooms are filled with all sorts of precious riches and valuables.***

Nobody stumbles on success. To achieve success in any endeavor, first of all, you need to grab a seat and create a plan.

Every towering building was, first of all, a plan on paper before its construction started.

Every hit TV production was first planned out adequately before filming began.

The earth at its beginning gives us clues to the fact that our creation was thoroughly thought through and planned stepwise by GOD even though He really didn't need to, seeing that He reports to absolutely no one. Still, He chose not to do things haphazardly, instead, He created all things according to their place in nature. The sea came to be before the animals who live in the sea. The firm ground came to be before the plants of the ground. The plants of the ground came to be before the animals that would need the plants and so forth. He planned everything to minute details in order to create both the order and the balance needed to have an optimally functional ecosystem in which all His creations thrive. How did the earth, which was in a previous state of void, become God's Success? **Through the power of planning**. God planned everything He made everything with keen deliberateness from the placement of the hairs on our head to the twists and turns of the lines on our palms and the hardness of the nails covering the top of our toes.

Planning shows how intentional you are about success.

If God did things according to details and plans, you have no excuse.

Enough of spiritual gimmicks and time–wasting, if your current approach to life and success is not working, you need to reconsider changing your plan or strategy.

The prodigal son of the Bible in Luke 15:17–19 planned his way out of lack and poverty to success and it sure worked for him:

> ***"But when he came to himself, he said, 'How many of my father's hired servants have bread enough and to spare, and I perish with hunger! I will arise and go to my father, and will say to him, "Father, I have sinned against heaven and before you, and I am no longer worthy to be called your son. Make me like one of your hired servants."'"***

We all know how the story panned out.

Here's a little story to further buttress the importance of planning:

In 1948, Yale University surveyed a particular graduating class. Only 3% knew what they wanted to do and wrote it down. Another 10% knew what they wanted to do but didn't write it down. The remaining 87% did neither. They believed they would survive along the way. "Whatever comes, anything goes"

25 years later, the first 3% who wrote down their plans had achieved 50–100% more than the 10% who knew their plans but never wrote them down. The other 87% were nowhere to be found.

Again, for the sake of your purpose, please grab a seat and plan.

No pilot ever takes off from the airport without a flight plan. No authority will let that aircraft go into the air. The flight plan must be clearly stated, submitted, and signed before the plane is allowed to fly. Even at that, the pilot must stay on course or else the ground control team would be in touch. This is a simple and straightforward allegorical reason why people who are not planners are not high flyers. *Only those with flight plans are allowed to fly.*

In order to arrive at your preferred destination, you need a map and a means. If your goals are worth pursuing, then they deserve a proper plan.

While planning, your goals must be set with certain fundamentals in mind which can be termed as 'the ABCs of Goal Setting'.

The ABCs of Goal Setting

A–Achievable: It must be doable even if it is innovative. For it to be doable, you may need to be flexible with your plans or your means of achieving your set goal.

B–Believable: It should stretch you but it should not be overwhelming.

C–Concrete: It must be a solid goal that is worth every bit of your lifetime that you're willing to invest into it.

Areas to set goals

To outline these, we will take cues from Luke 2:52–"And Jesus increased in wisdom and stature, and in favor with God and men."

Set career goals: Jesus advanced greatly in wisdom. You can't advance except you invest in building your skill sets and competencies. To increase in wisdom, expand your mind with relevant knowledge and wisdom every day. Listen to inspiring audios and read good books. Be dissatisfied about remaining at the same level of intellect. Master your craft by gaining wisdom daily in your chosen field. Aim to become an authority therein in the space of an allotted period of time.

Set health goals: Jesus grew in stature. Prevention, they say, is better than cure and there is nothing truer than this. Do your physicals! Keep fit and exercise. Eat healthily.

Set spiritual goals: Jesus increased in favor with God. Set goals that will determine things like how many times you will fast monthly, how much added time you need to commit to your devotion with God, what you will give to God yearly, how many people you will bring to church monthly etc.

Set relationship goals: Jesus grew in favor with men. Invest in your social life, starting with family. Set specific goals such as marital goals, goals around how you raise your children, family bonding goals, vacations etc. Also, set quality networking goals that foster the growth of your life's purpose while you simultaneously become that go–to friend yourself.

Set financial goals: Jesus and his disciples had a financial 'purse'. At the last supper, the disciples thought Judas was instructed by Jesus to carry on their plan to give to the poor from their financial purse in his custody. Have a detailed budget, outlining your income streams, expenditure, savings, and investments. I, for one, see tithes and offerings as being planted and not being spent. Therefore, I term those as seeds or kingdom investments and not expenditure. Set goals on how to get out of debt (if there are any), how to grow your earnings, and how to multiply your streams of income.

Whatever you do, **plan.**

Planning separates the achiever from the mediocre, the extraordinary persons from the ordinary people. Planning is critical to the success of any man's life and endeavors.

Planning and purpose go hand–in–hand. **Purpose is dead without a plan**. This is because Purpose is driven by Planning.

A plan reveals the picture of the future. Any business that is not well planned will fail. Same for any life. If you don't know where you are going and how to get there, you will end up anywhere and eventually, nowhere.

Every building begins with a plan, except if it is a valueless building. Hebrews 3:4 says, "For every house is built by someone, but He who built all things is God." You must have heard people say, "We built our business....". It has to be built and if it has to be built, it must have a plan.

Planning is a key attribute of a good manager of resources. Good management, in turn, guarantees good results. Money not well managed will be squandered. Life itself, if not well managed, will be a waste.

Anything that must grow must first be well managed or put under good management.

In time management, the process from Purpose (ideation) to Delivery (final results) looks like this:

Purpose–Planning–Program–Pursuit–Delivery

Once Planning is missing, the process can be stuck at the purpose or ideation phase for life.

In a nutshell, *What Is Planning?* It is a plainly described, step–by–step approach to accomplish a goal. Planning puts needful order to the available priorities into order to accomplish a task. Planning is a spelt–out process of action in the quest to fulfill a dream.

No one succeeds by accident. Only a self–conceited failure can boldly define the success of others as mere luck. *Shallow minds think of success as happenstance, great men think of success as a cause from an effect.*

Raw materials for achieving great planning

What then makes up a great plan?

Rational, logical and analytical thinking is what makes for good planning. Every great planner must be a great thinker. Success is largely the product of strategic thinking.

The Bible, in Proverbs 24:3–5 AMP, summarily ascribes the future of every endeavor to the power of wise planning, understanding and knowledge. This goes to show that getting common sense and engaging all available facts and up–to–date information is also a critical phase of planning.

If you are not committed to putting in the mental work, you will end up with menial work.

Make your brain work while you create plans. While you sweat it out on the drawing board working up a plan, your mental capability improves and develops. As you continue to flesh up your plans, you begin to see things in the light of several perspectives and your heart begins to enlarge towards the realm of endless possibilities.

Ready to begin to plan? These are the steps to take:

Steps to take while planning

Set a definite goal: Nothing becomes dynamic until it is first specific. Ask precise questions like “How much money?”, “What type of house?”, “What type of job?”

Set a deadline: Set a definite time. Ask yourself, “When will I achieve it?” Deadlines help you define when each task is due. It helps achieve steady progress. The production of this book itself entailed creating different milestones with deadliness, helping the team stay on top of the different tasks to successfully publish it at the set time. See deadlines as your accountability partner. Stick close to it!

Write down your goal: Seeing your goal leap out of your mind and written in black and white is one step towards its accomplishment. The Scripture says in Habakkuk 2:2–“Then the Lord answered me and said: “Write the vision and make it plain on tablets, that he may run who reads it.” Just as iterated, write it so clear enough that it can be understood without being explained.

Develop a process to achieve your goal: Write down a step–by–step process. Ask, “How can you achieve it from where you are today?” Planning like this gets you ready for the journey. Afterall, the more prepared you are, the early you can spot bottlenecks and potential hiccups, giving it a smoother sail to the set goal

Determine the price that it will cost you: Achieving goals will cost you something. What will you give in exchange? You can't get something for nothing. Life responds to value and it gives a corresponding return for value. What you get is dependent on what you give out and this is directly based on the principle of sowing and reaping.

Visualize the success of the plan: This is why building constructors make a miniature–sized structure of what they intend to create. Put the picture up of the plan in its finished state. The time will come when you don't have to look at it anymore. It will become tangible to you and your spirit will pick it up as though it were already in existence. With proper steps taken, before long, your faith will become sight.

Failing to plan, in itself, is a foolproof strategy on planning to fail.

In all that you do on your path to success, don't fail to plan.

LET'S SAY THIS TOGETHER:

"I am a planner and an achiever like God is a planner and achiever. I follow through on my periodic plans and I trust the process"

CHAPTER 7

LAW OF PROCESS

"The Lord your God will drive those nations out ahead of you* little by little. *You will not clear them away all at once, otherwise the wild animals would multiply too quickly for you."

Deuteronomy 7:22 (NLT)

Before we proceed to tackle the issue of process, understand that the meal called process is best served with a chilled glass of patience. The virtue called 'patience' is the most important asset to have when it comes to the Law of Process. The very fact that you arrived at this page in this book is tied to the fact that you patiently consumed the content letter by letter, word after word, a sentence and then another, one paragraph following the other, flipping page after page. Now, unto the thing called Process.

The Author of Process

The Author of Process is God Himself. Even though He is the ALMIGHTY, God is a stickler for process.

He not only initiated the process but He subjected Himself to that same process to set a precedent. He didn't choose to skip the class just because He's the teacher. God envisioned 6 billion people on earth but He started with one man and then, a woman. If He created all 6 billion people at once (and yes, He had the power to), it would have been extremely chaotic. Just imagine it!

What were the factors in between the 2 people created in the beginning and 6 billion people and counting as we have it today? **Process** and **Time**.

When it comes to success, God understands that the capacity of man must be built progressively. To Him, every moment and phase in His making of a man into a success is equally important. He would not deem it fit to give you everything you'll ever have all at once so the blessing does not become a curse and does you great damage instead of good.

If a woman gets pregnant today, the growing child in her

womb requires an ample amount of time to mature before it can survive outside the womb. Even Jesus, the second person in the Trinity, upon His arrival on earth came as a newborn baby fully formed in the womb over a period of time. He had to wait to grow even though He could have shown up on our planet as a grown man. Aside from the process of creation, the coming of Jesus as a baby is another indicator that God honors the Law of Process and so should we.

Your dream is to become a Medical Doctor but you would need time to grow and go through school for another 18 years starting at Elementary School.

This is the reason why I can be bold to say that the city, land or industry you couldn't conquer initially will be subdued by you eventually IF YOU DON'T QUIT GETTING BETTER. DON'T YOU EVER QUIT because your dream is not happening all at once. WAIT FOR IT!

As business leader John C. Maxwell commented on The Law of Process in his bestselling book, *The 21 Irrefutable Laws of Leadership* saying that the routines and tasks you make time for each day are what will eventually make a success out of both yourself and your business.

He also rightly noted saying: "See what a person is doing every day, day after day, and you'll know who that person is and what he or she is becoming." I couldn't agree more.

Success is, therefore, an aggregate of daily inputs. Progress in

Life is an accumulation of daily improvements.

Trust the Process

The best professionals in every industry today all began as novices. Don't be discouraged by your growing phases or processes. You can only walk as an adult today because you never gave up on walking as a toddler.

Put in the work, day after day, time after time, learning after disappointments, rising after falls, growing and growing, getting better and better and you will evolve into the fullness of the vision you see for your life. Keep going! Keep growing!

LET'S SAY THIS TOGETHER:

"I'm on my journey, I'm on my way. The process–I'll patiently follow, the price–I'll patiently pay.

Ready or not, Success, here I come!"

CHAPTER 8

LAW OF PRICE

"The good and the great are only separated by the willingness to sacrifice."
–Kareem Abdul–Jabbar

Nothing in life is free. There is a VALUE attached to everything of Value. This VALUE is its PRICE

The Holy Book is not negligent about the law of price and pricing. It is strewn all over the book as everyday life is in full view as it is here:

"But the others replied, 'We don't have enough

for all of us. Go to a shop and buy some for yourselves."

Matthew 25:9

Life is transactional in nature and everything of value comes at a **COST** either to you or someone else.

Universal constants about the Law of Price

When it comes to the Law of Price in relation to success, there are certain constants to be mindful of no matter who or where you are:

The Price must be paid: To succeed in life, you must be willing to make sacrifices. Some people think they can coast along in life and still accomplish greatness. Nothing can be farther from the truth. As the saying goes, "there is no free lunch (even in Freetown)". Someone paid for it some way or another. If you wait for someone to always pay for your meal, you will starve. You must be driven to pay your own bills. Anyone with a true heart of responsibility gets uncomfortable when others perpetually foot their bills.

The Price must be paid all the time: There is a phenomenon referred to as the 'destination disease'. It is an erroneous belief system that postulates that once a great accomplishment or outstanding goal is attained, there is no longer a need to grow or improve. This limiting mindset applies in countless situations. Whether in growing a business or earning a degree, reaching a desired position at work or receiving a particular award, the destination disease is easy to catch. This negative mindset makes us think that we can stop working, stop striving and stop paying the price, and yet still reach our potential. Unfortunately, the day you stop growing, you put a limiting cap on your potential. Destination disease is as dangerous for a team as it is for any individual. It is crucial to remember that there is no other price for continuous success than continued hard work itself. President Dwight D. Eisenhower knew this truth, which was why he said, "There are no victories at bargain prices." If you want to reach your potential, you must never let up, no matter what happens. Make up your mind to give in to neither the pains of disappointment nor a sense of utmost achievement.

The Price to be paid increases for every new stage of success: It costs something to advance or to go up, it costs something to stay up and it sure costs more to keep advancing. Persistent winning requires a high price which keeps on going higher and staying on top requires even higher levels of sacrifice. Have you ever thought of how many companies stay at the top of *Forbes* magazine's lists for a decade? There are very few because the higher you are, the more the price you have to pay to make improvements to retain your height and go even higher. Whether as an athlete or as a student, for every sphere of life in which you desire improvement, you must pay the price by training harder and learning smarter. You may not think working harder than you already are in the present moment is possible, but if you want to remain at the top, you will have to.

When most people quit during a challenge, they don't give up at the beginning. They stop halfway. Millions of people who set New Year Resolutions resort to this year–in, year–out.

While the truth is that nobody sets out on a mission with the purpose of quitting; the actual problem is the mindset they uphold during the challenge. This mindset is culled from the mistaken belief that a time will come when attaining success will miraculously get easier along the way. The truth is that life rarely works that way. There are no shortcuts to any place worth going to. In paying the price all the way to the end, you must encourage yourself, self–motivate, and keep the vision unshaken in your heart. As you keep working towards your purpose, you must keep enlarging in capacity to handle the good, the bad, and the in–betweens.

Does everyone truly have a price?

There's an age–long notion that "everybody has a price". This connotes that there is a school of thought which believes that everyone's voice, conscience, sense of morality, sound judgment, body, truth or even faith can be bought at a price that varies from person to person. Some people even boast of being able to buy people over for all the wrong reasons and evil intentions.

I'd like to ask you one question; *do you have a price?* Think long and hard about it.

Is there an amount of money on earth or certain privileges that can make you renounce the things you hold dear or in the highest esteem today?

While you think of that, please remember Gehazi the servant of Elisha and also remember Judas Iscariot, the disciple of Jesus Christ. Think about the privileges they had and the far greater benefits they would have received if they refused to be bought.

Remember Joseph who was enticed by Potiphar's wife. Even though he was blackmailed and eventually sent to prison, he was still on his path to purpose because he refused to be bought. Can you imagine what would have become of him if he succumbed to the luring of Mrs. Potiphar? He would most likely never have known the way to the palace, let alone become the King's adviser and Prime Minister of Egypt. We can never know what would have become of him because he remained resolute and stood his ground for the right thing.

Above all, think of our Lord Jesus, who in his life as a human was faced with several trials aimed at getting Him to sell out on the purpose why He was sent to the earth. From the start of his earthly ministry, the devil, in a three–part temptation, dared Him to prove that He was indeed the Son of God and then tried to buy over Jesus for a price, as seen in Luke 4:1–12. Up until the last hours before fulfilling His purpose at Calvary, He was taunted by people who mocked Him while hanging on the cross (for their sakes). These people, as well as one of the thieves hung beside His cross, taunted Him to prove that He was truly the Son of God as He claimed to be. People, this was after Jesus had been "slain since the foundation of the world". The decision had been made and the deed had been concluded before time began and when time began, circumstances began to rear their ugly heads in an attempt to dissuade Him from fulfilling it.

It's the same for you. If the devil could come for Jesus who He knew was the Son of God, he certainly will dangle a price in your face as well. When this time comes, remember this line of this book and never forget that your purpose and success is already a God–written story scripted before time began. Selling out for a price, no matter the price tag, will literally be your own undoing.

Take courage from Hebrews 12:1–2 (NLT)–

> ***"Therefore, since we are surrounded by such a huge crowd of witnesses to the life of faith, let us strip off every weight that slows us down, especially the sin that so easily trips us up. And let us run with endurance the race God has set before us. We do this by keeping our eyes on Jesus, the champion who initiates and perfects our faith.Because of the joy awaiting him, he endured the cross, disregarding its shame. Now he is seated in the place of honor beside God's throne."***

Allow me to say this in full caps.

THE PRIZE OF YOUR PURPOSE IS FAR MORE PRECIOUS THAN THE PRICE YOU NEED TO PAY FOR IT.

THE PRICE YOU NEED PAY FOR YOUR PURPOSE IS FAR LESS COSTLY THAN THE LOSS YOU WILL INCUR BY SELLING OUT ON IT!

2 Corinthians 4:17 further explains this:

> ***"For our light affliction, which is for a moment, is working for us a far more exceeding and eternal weight of glory, while we do not look at the things which are seen, but at the things which are not seen. For the things which are seen are temporary, but the things which are not seen are eternal."***

The Law of Price is made for processes and not for persons or personal value. Never sell out on your personal values for some loose change no matter the amount. You are God's inestimable asset and investment. Your value will continue to go up as you keep discovering your purpose. If you had been bought for a cheap price, you'd quickly realize that you sold yourself cheaply. Stay grounded! Take the pains to pay the price for your journey along the path of purpose.

Refuse to emulate neither of the two kinds of people who violate the Law of the Price–those who don't think success comes at a price nor model after those who realize it comes at a price but are not willing to pay it. You need to answer the question, 'When should I start paying the price, now or later?'

No one on the mountain top fell there. They climbed all the way to the top. It's best to make up your mind to believe that success will always cost you something.

Find out what your quest for success will cost you and surrender your will to pay it no matter what shows up on the journey! Your life's success is a prize worth the price!

LET'S SAY THIS TOGETHER:

"Whatever is written on the price tag to my success, I am willing to pay for it. Though it may not come easy, it will be well worth it—this is my new perception about success."

CHAPTER 9

LAW OF PERCEPTION

"And she said unto her husband, Behold now, I perceive that this is a holy man of God, which passeth by us continually."

2 Kings 4:9

Thinking through the passage above, you'd want to ask what exactly made the woman conclude that Elisha was a holy man of God. This was even before he performed any miracles before her eyes.

If we flipped that perception on its head, it would read, "And she said unto her husband, Behold now, I perceive that this is an unclean and devilish man, which passeth by us continually."

If the Prophet Elisha had sent the wrong message across for any reason, it wouldn't matter whether he carried the mantle of Elijah or not, he would have been put at arm's length by the woman and her family. He wouldn't have had a place to turn into as he journeyed in that region and the woman wouldn't have gotten her miraculous son through the word of God on Elisha's lips. Things would have been very different.

How you are perceived determines how you are treated and how easily and quickly your purpose finds expression. This is because the pervading perception about you determines how people relate to you and why they do. It dictates who can receive from or give to you and what they receive from or give to you.

Perception speaks for you even before you open your mouth to speak for yourself. Your perception can either 'get your foot in the door' or turn you far away from the building.

People who function in the entertainment space and popular 'pop' culture understand the power of perception and this is why they pay great attention to selling the perceivable image of the performer as much as they would want to sell the talent of the performer. This is because they understand how the human mind functions. They capitalize on the fact that the human attention span, in such a fast–paced world as ours, is about 8 seconds and it keeps decreasing as years go by and as global advancement increases. Therefore, they go straight to the point when building the idea perceivable about a person. No mixed perceptions, only the real deal they intend to 'sell' from the get–go.

Perception is your teaser or promo copy about your person while your entire self is the full movie. Perception is that invisible PR person who goes ahead to sell your persona way before you arrive at a place or before a person.

Perception can either make or murder your personality. People can either buy into your person or be totally put off by you based on the perception they have about you.

A constantly denting perception can damage years of building a great persona the same way one rightly placed perception over a period of time can do you a whole world of good.

By the power of perception, you either short–change or put a premium value on yourself.

Nobody is born with the perception that rules the most of their adult life. We are all born as blank pages when it comes to the matter of perception. Perception is created over a period just like a daily, monthly, weekly, or yearly deposit that accrues with time. This is why you must be deliberate about creating a perception about yourself that matches your personality, and by and large, your purpose.

A poor presentation of yourself might make people have the

wrong idea about you and not understand your purpose, even though it is God given. Yes, it's that serious. Apparently, God needs you to be deliberate about your perception as well, in order not to waste His investment of purpose in your life.

To do this, you must pay premium attention to certain 'perception points'.

Key Perception Points

These perception points include:

Appearance: Dress the way you seek to be addressed. This is not in any way to assert that you must pay more attention to your appearance than the content or intellect of your mind, however, to attract the necessary people to the content of a product, the package must be made to create the necessary appeal to attract those people to itself. I'm not saying you must break the bank or fake an appearance but have a sense of style with what you can afford per time. Let your appearance match your purpose and tell the world that you're a success going somewhere to happen. When it comes to dressing, a little attention to detail changes everything. People notice when thought is put into combining an outfit. Pay attention to your personal details; smell nice, have a neat haircut, keep clean nails, keep your smile bright and fresh. I don't know about you but I love the smell of the interior of a brand–new car. That's how certain appearances also appeal to people. Fresh and clean. Invest into your appearance and you're sure to reap from this investment soonest. Even you would feel great about yourself and purpose as you continue to do this.

Carriage: You may have the appearance but you can wield it very, very poorly. From gesticulations to stance to the way you walk, your carriage says a lot about you. Interpretation of your carriage by others determines whether or not you can be referred to as a person with **presence**. Learn how to equate the kind of aura that you let off as a person with your personality such that it compliments your purpose. Don't carry yourself as a fearful person when you are actually dauntless. Let your charisma be a foretaste of your person and let it attract people to your purpose.

Speech: This refers to both your in–person verbal communication skills as well as your virtual communication skills. In a media–driven age like this, none of the two outweighs the other. As much as you pay attention to sending across the right message with your in–person communication skills, you must not undermine your virtual persona with contradictory communication. Make sure they are both in sync and saying the same things the same way. Let them always align with your purpose as distinctly as possible to prevent people from having the wrong perceptions, and eventually, the wrong *expectations* about you. Just so people wouldn't get things twisted and expect more from him than he could give, the forerunner of Jesus–John the Baptist clarified that he wasn't the Christ. Also, be careful with the *tone* of your communication. Watch *what* you say and watch *how* you say it. Be clear and intentional about the perception you want to spread about yourself and your purpose using your communication. Mean what you say and say what you mean.

Tools for intentional perception creation:

Conversations: Join conversations and make contributions in line with your purpose. Sometimes people won't know what you carry until you open your mouth.

Interact: No man is an island. Purpose is not self–serving. Until you interact with other people, your purpose will probably remain in a potential state or a state of inertia. At best, you will continue to imagine what could be until you begin to interact with, serve and learn from others.

A clause I must add about perception is this: Do not try too hard or force anyone to believe a certain perception about you, especially if they choose to believe a wrong and unhealthy perception. Stay true to yourself and to your purpose as you continue to evolve day after day. They will have no option other than to catch up with the true version of you if you keep at it on your journey, living in purpose.

LET'S SAY THIS TOGETHER:

"Henceforth, I will be extra intentional about reflecting a clear perception about my person across all my relationships for the sake of my purpose"

CHAPTER 10

LAW OF RELATIONSHIPS

People are your greatest resource on earth.

Everything we will ever need to succeed is in the hands of people.

> ***Give, and it shall be given unto you: good measure, pressed down, shaken together, and running over will be put (by men) into your bosom. For with the same measure that you use, it will be measured back to you.***
>
> Luke 6:38

The KJV version quotes the Lord Jesus in the same verse as above saying, "...and running over, shall *men* give into your bosom."

Not angels. Men. God designed it that way.

In other words, your Network determines your Net worth. You cannot be more successful than the worth of the people in your network. Your ability to build relationships is a critical key to your success. Building relationships is, however, a skill that has to be learned and carried out purposefully.

The basis on which the law of relationships functions is this: **we attract who we are.**

Honing great relationships starts with attracting the right people. However, you cannot attract who you are not.

What is the kind of energy you let off as a person? When people have encounters with you, they must feel the right kind of energy. Nobody wants to be around Mr. Grump Bad Vibes or Ms. Pessimism: Nothing works!

Energies attract each other because they resonate at the same wavelength. The more positive energy we give, the more we'll receive. The same is true for negativity.

Grumpiness attracts grumpiness. Passion attracts passion. Rage attracts rage.

Becoming a Person of Positivity

How do you become a person of positivity?

1. **Love yourself:** The more you love yourself, the more positivity you tend to ooze. To breed healthy relationships, you must, first of all, focus less on your insecurities, identify your best qualities, and put the spotlight on those. We are all works–in–progress so you need to appreciate the good in you to be able to give some out and get goodness in return. Love and value yourself in order to change the way you see life. Be kind to yourself. Give yourself some self–respect; this comes from knowing your worth. Know your worth/ your value and add some tax to that. Give yourself a treat every now and then. It beams cheer and positive vibes right out of your person.

2. **Love others:** See the best in people. Invest and generously give to people. This, of course, can never happen until you love yourself. You cannot even truly love your family and friends if you do not love yourself. The message of Galatians 5:14 is repeated all over scripture; "For all the law is fulfilled in one word, even in this: "You shall love your neighbor as yourself."

3. **Be genuine:** People can identify when one is being phony. Whatever you do, keep it real. Don't make a show out of caring for yourself or others without really meaning it. At the end of it all, life turns out weightless

and meaningless if everything was done under a guise or in false pretense.

In relationships, instead of accentuating the worst in a person or situation, choose to energize and amplify positive qualities. Let your *aim* be to influence people towards constructive transformation. The motivation should not be to flatter, to play nice, to be 'politically correct' or ignore intuitive red flags neither is it to deny someone's dark side or placate abusers. Your goal is to mine the gold in positive relationships and to magnify the potentials and possibilities in difficult relationships. Let people be eternally thankful that they met you in their lifetime. **However, when relationships turn toxic, you need to know when to let go for the good of all.**

Use your words wisely in relationships. Words are the most inexpensive yet powerful and dynamic tools in relationships. With words, you should heal, not hurt. Build with words, do not tear apart. Scriptures say we should give grace to our hearers whenever we open our mouths to say a thing. To give grace means to edify, to build up, to cheer up, and encourage.

To build relationships, you must be willing to appraise people positively when they put in effort. If you want to connect with someone, notice their potential and let them know you think of them as assets. We all desire to have the goodness in us acknowledged and if we desire this, we must be willing to give it.

The Most Important Relationship of all

Above all, you must honor your relationship with God by making sure that it has utmost priority. God is *your* Father. Let that sink in. You are a child of God. While on earth, the Lord Jesus took His relationship with God so seriously that the Pharisees called Him a blasphemer. Jesus was dedicated, committed and devoted to His relationship with God both in the public eye and in His private moments. He knew His success on earth was fully dependent on His relationship with His Father in heaven. Your relationship with God must reflect in your relationships with people and not make them wonder if you know Him at all.

1 John 4:20–21(NLT) declares:

> ***"If someone says, "I love God," but hates a fellow believer, that person is a liar; for if we don't love people we can see, how can we love God, whom we cannot see? And he has given us this command: Those who love God must also love their fellow believers."***

If you're not yet born again, you are not yet a child of God. That means the relationship you have with God is a Creator–Creation affiliation. You are surely missing a lot and God cannot wait to have you in His big family. Becoming a child of God is really important to your long–term success both in this life and in eternity after this life is all over. It's pretty simple as well. Just say this prayer without a doubt in your heart:

Lord Jesus, I come to you as I am. Forgive my sins today and make me brand new again. I accept you into my heart, and confess Jesus as my Lord and Savior. I am now a child of God, Amen.

LET'S SAY THIS TOGETHER:

"I appreciate the gift of the people in my life therefore I make sure to invest in my relationships with intentionally uplifting words and deeds."

CHAPTER 11

LAW OF APPRECIATION

Appreciation, in terms of being appreciative means to be grateful or thankful for something or to someone.

While on our journey on the earth, we experience the unmerited blessings of God in many ways than we can measure. The finger of God can be found in it all, from big deal successes to the everyday functionality of our being. The fact that you can acquire, read and understand the content of this book as well as prop yourself up or lie down, hold this book, flip the pages and close the book when you're all done–all that is actually a long chain of miracles. Until you cannot do one or more of these 'simple' activities unassisted, you probably will not know the extent to which you have been helped by God.

You simply don't know what you have until it's gone and irrecoverable.

If you want to be honest, there are thousands of ways that God blesses us daily both according to what we ask or think and according to what we do not remember to ask for or think about.

Indeed, Psalms 68:19 holds true–"Blessed be the Lord,

Who daily loads us with benefits, The God of our salvation! Selah"

As we continue on our earthly journeys, a lot of times, we witness the success of others. This often happens in the field of our pursuit or in a way that matches the desires of our hearts for ourselves.

Our response to this must not be from a place of envy, impatience, unhealthy comparison, hatred or snide remarks. We must, instead, celebrate with others with understanding, having a mindset that their testimonies are our prophecies.

I know we have read the scriptures in Romans 12:15 that say, "rejoice with those who rejoice, and weep with those who weep." Quite frankly, waiting for your own success or your own breakthrough may be somewhat tedious but responding to the success of others with malicious intent will certainly not hasten your results or the processes behind your success. Impatience might drive you toward cutting corners and snide remarks will only poison your idea of how success is achieved. If you eventually arrive at some kind of success after cutting corners from a warped mindset about success, you will not be proud to share your success story and no one will learn anything useful from your purpose.

It is only wise that you stay focused on your lane as you continue to work at your dreams. Only that really adds up to deliver your desires. Keep at it! You're closer to breaking through than you were at the beginning of your journey. You are much closer than you think!

Keep your heart pure and your hopes high for the arrival of your big break and when it arrives, yours will be the latest success story to amaze the world.

Living a life of Appreciation is possible

How?

Begin to make a habit of appreciating these people groups:

Yourself: This simply cannot be overemphasized. Whether you choose to believe it or not, you're stuck with you for life. Who then should be your biggest fan? Make a decision to be your biggest cheerleader! Live to celebrate **YOU**! Give yourself a pat on the back, a hi–5, or a hug daily. Breed a healthy self–esteem by investing in affirmations that speak to the greatness that you are and by living those affirmations out in your everyday life. Carry an unshakable God–esteem by focusing on what God says about you and your purpose. When it comes to thinking about yourself or meditating about your future, you (of all people) should not be caught thinking small or bad. You would be doing all your hard work a great disservice. Think good, BIG thoughts about yourself that will point you to the direction of your grand and glorious destiny. Tell yourself, "(insert your name), you're one heck of a phenomenon! Lord knows that there are 5,999,999 billion people that cannot wait to meet the beautiful soul that you are!" or say something like, "You put in so much extra effort this past week! I owe you a sweet cheat day". Appreciate yourself some more.

God: He deserves it all. Testify to His awesomeness towards you and yours. Give towards the expansion of His kingdom on earth. Praise Him. Praise God in retrospect and praise Him in anticipation. Praising God is a major way of showing you appreciate Him. You can do this by song or just by your heartfelt words. From your lips to His ears. Praise never fails to get God's attention. God inhabits the praise of His people, says Proverbs 22:3. Besides, the scripture says in Psalm 67:5–6, "Let the peoples praise You, O God; Let all the peoples praise You. Then the earth shall yield her increase; God, our own God, shall bless us." Have you put in the work but it looks like the results are delayed? Praise God. Praise will bring the increase.

The **PEOPLE** in your life and the little/awesome things they do: Appreciate the things people do for you. They alone can tell you just how much doing that for you cost them.

Keep words that portray gratitude and elicit the feeling of appreciation handy.

The successes of **OTHERS**: Be genuinely happy for and with people. It is often said that when God blesses your neighbor, then God must be in the neighborhood. Celebrate the achievements of others on the way to yours.

LET'S SAY THIS TOGETHER:

"Thank you, God, for all you do for me and all mine. From today, I maintain an attitude of gratitude and appreciation till it becomes my default practice and a part of my character."

CHAPTER 12

LAW OF PRACTICE

This is by far the most important of all the Laws written in this book.

Go on and put all you have learned thus far to practice over and over again at different phases of your life.

1 Timothy 4:15 (NLT)–

> ***"Give your complete attention to these matters. Throw yourself into your tasks so that everyone will see your progress."***

My favorite synonym for the word "Unstuck" is to be free and this is because he whom the Son of God has set free is free indeed.

You're UNSTUCK and UNSTOPPABLE!

Skyward to Success! Godspeed!

www.ingramcontent.com/pod-product-compliance
Ingram Content Group UK Ltd.
Pitfield, Milton Keynes, MK11 3LW, UK
UKHW062256290726
14090UKWH00017B/721

9 798330 305117